Samsung Galaxy Buds3 Pro

User Guide

Discover Comprehensive Features, Setup instructions and Helpful tips

Sheryll H. Elias

Copyright

Disclaimer

Table of Contents

INTRODUCTION

The Samsung Galaxy Buds3 Pro is a premium true wireless earbud designed to elevate your audio experience. With its sleek design, cutting-edge features, and seamless integration into the Samsung ecosystem, it caters to both audiophiles and everyday users. This user guide is crafted to help you maximize the potential of your Galaxy Buds3 Pro, providing detailed instructions and tips for a superior experience.

Product Overview

The Galaxy Buds3 Pro represents a significant upgrade in Samsung's audio lineup, offering a combination of enhanced sound quality, user-centric features, and innovative design. These earbuds are tailored to meet the needs of various lifestyles, from professional environments to fitness and entertainment settings.

Key Features

- **Advanced Audio Performance:** Equipped with custom-tuned dual drivers and support for 24-bit Hi-Fi sound, the Galaxy Buds3 Pro delivers a rich and dynamic audio experience. The wide soundstage and customizable equalizer settings ensure an immersive listening journey.

- **Active Noise Cancelation (ANC) and Transparency Mode**: ANC effectively reduces ambient noise, while the Transparency Mode allows users to remain aware of their surroundings with clarity, perfect for commuting or multitasking.

- **Smart Integration and AI Features:** Features like real-time language translation, neck stretch reminders, and seamless device switching offer a modern and intelligent listening experience, particularly for Samsung Galaxy users.

- **360 Audio and Spatial Sound:** The 360 Audio feature with Dolby Head Tracking technology provides an immersive surround sound experience, making media consumption more engaging.

- **Durability and Portability:** With an IP57 rating for dust and water resistance, the earbuds are built to withstand daily wear and occasional exposure to the elements. Compact and lightweight, they are easy to carry and store.

Benefits of the Galaxy Buds3 Pro

- **Enhanced Productivity:** The seamless switching between devices and intuitive touch controls allow you to stay connected without interruptions.

- **Comfort and Style:** Designed for all-day use, the earbuds offer a snug fit and come in elegant finishes to match your personal style.

- **Health and Wellness:** The neck stretch reminders add a unique wellness feature, promoting better posture during extended use.

- **Versatile Usage**: Whether you're at work, at the gym, or relaxing at home, the Galaxy Buds3 Pro adapts to your needs with long battery life and customizable sound profiles.

BOX CONTENTS

The Samsung Galaxy Buds3 Pro package is carefully designed to include all essential components required for a seamless setup and use. Below is a detailed list of the contents:

1. Samsung Galaxy Buds3 Pro: These are the main wireless earbuds designed to deliver high-quality audio. They feature advanced sound technology, including an independently controlled woofer and tweeter for a rich audio experience. They also come with adaptive noise control to help you stay immersed in your music or calls.

2. Charging Case: The charging case serves a dual function. It stores the earbuds when not in use and charges them, extending their battery life. The case itself can be charged using the included USB-C cable, ensuring your earbuds are always ready to go.

3. USB-C Cable: This cable is used to charge the charging case. You can connect it to any USB-C compatible charger or a computer. The USB-C standard is known for its fast charging capabilities, ensuring your case and earbuds charge quickly.

4. Ear Tips (Small, Medium, Large): These silicone ear tips come in three different sizes to ensure a comfortable and secure fit for various ear sizes. The right fit is crucial for comfort and optimal sound quality, as well as effective noise cancellation. The medium tips are usually pre-applied, but you can switch to the small or large tips based on your preference.

5. User Manual: The user manual provides detailed instructions on how to set up and use your Galaxy Buds3 Pro. It includes information on pairing the earbuds with your devices, using the touch controls, and troubleshooting common issues. It's a handy guide to help you get the most out of your new earbuds.

Optional Accessories:

The inclusion of optional accessories like a Wireless Charging Pad and a Carrying Pouch can vary depending on the region and the specific bundle you purchase. Here's a bit more about these accessories:

1. Wireless Charging Pad: This accessory allows you to charge the case and earbuds wirelessly, providing a convenient and cable-free charging experience. Simply place the case on the pad to start charging.

2. Carrying Pouch: A soft pouch designed for storing and carrying the case and earbuds. It offers additional protection, especially useful when traveling, to keep your earbuds safe from scratches and damage.

These accessories are not always included in every box and may be part of special bundles or promotions. It's a good idea to check the specific contents listed for the bundle you are considering purchasing to see if these optional accessories are included.

GETTING STARTED

How to Charge the Samsung Galaxy Buds3 Pro and the Charging Case

Charging the Samsung Galaxy Buds3 Pro and its case is essential to maintain optimal performance. Here are steps, along with tips for safe and efficient charging:

Charging the Earbuds

1. Using the Charging Case:

- Place the Earbuds in the Case: Insert the earbuds into their respective slots in the charging case. Ensure they are properly aligned and the charging contacts are touching.

- Close the Case: Close the lid of the charging case to start charging the earbuds. The case will automatically begin charging the earbuds.

Charging the Charging Case

1. Using a USB-C Cable:

- Connect the Cable: Plug the USB-C end of the cable into the charging port on the back of the case.

- Connect to a Power Source: Plug the other end of the cable into a USB-C compatible charger or a computer.

- Charging Indicator: The LED indicator on the case will light up to show that it is charging. The color of the LED indicates the battery level (e.g., red for low, yellow for medium, green for fully charged).

2. Using a Wireless Charging Pad (if available):

- Place the Case on the Pad: Position the charging case on the wireless charging pad with the lid facing up.

- Ensure Proper Alignment: Make sure the case is centered on the pad for optimal charging.

- Charging Indicator: The LED indicator on the case will light up to show that it is charging wirelessly.

Charging Times

Earbuds: Approximately 1 hour for a full charge inside the case.

Case: Around 2 hours with a USB-C cable; wireless charging may take longer.

Fast Charging: A quick 5-minute charge provides up to 1 hour of playback.

Tips for Safe and Efficient Charging

1. Use Original Accessories: Always use the provided USB-C cable or a Samsung-approved wireless charger to ensure compatibility, efficient charging and avoid damage.

2. Avoid Overcharging: Once the earbuds and case are fully charged, disconnect them from the power source to prevent overcharging, which can reduce battery lifespan.

3. Keep the Charging Contacts Clean: Regularly clean the charging contacts on both the earbuds and the case with a dry, soft cloth to ensure a good connection.

4. Avoid Extreme Temperatures: Avoid charging the earbuds and case in extremely hot or humid environments, as this can damage the battery and its performance.

5. Monitor Charging: Keep an eye on the charging indicators to know when the devices are fully charged. This helps in maintaining the battery health over time.

6. Check Power Sources: Use a wall adapter with a 5V output for optimal charging. High-voltage chargers can damage the battery.

First-Time Setup

Steps for setting up your Samsung Galaxy Buds3 Pro for the first time, including powering on and pairing with a device:

Step 1: Charge the Earbuds and Case

Before setting up, ensure that both the earbuds and the charging case are fully charged. This ensures they have enough power for the setup process.

Step 2: Power On the Earbuds

1. Open the Charging Case: Place the earbuds inside the charging case and close the lid. This will automatically power on the earbuds.

2. Remove the Earbuds: Open the case and take out the earbuds. They should automatically enter pairing mode.

Step 3: Download the Galaxy Wearable App

1. Install the App: Download and install the Galaxy Wearable app from the Google Play Store (for Android devices) or the App Store (for iOS devices).

2. Open the App: Launch the Galaxy Wearable app on your device.

Step 4: Pairing with a Device

1. Enable Bluetooth: Ensure Bluetooth is enabled on your smartphone or tablet.

2. Open the Charging Case: With the earbuds inside, open the charging case. This will trigger a pairing request on your device.

3. Follow On-Screen Instructions: A pop-up should appear on your device. Tap "Connect" and follow the on-screen instructions to complete the pairing process.

Alternative Pairing Method

If the automatic pairing doesn't work, you can manually pair the earbuds:

1. Press the Connect Button: Open the charging case and press the connect button located on the bottom of the case for at least 3 seconds.

2. Select the Earbuds: Go to the Bluetooth settings on your device, find "Galaxy Buds3 Pro" in the list of available devices, and select it to pair.

Step 5: Customize Settings

1. Open the Galaxy Wearable App: Once paired, open the Galaxy Wearable app to customize your earbuds' settings.

2. Adjust Preferences: You can adjust various settings such as touch controls, noise cancellation, and sound profiles to suit your preferences.

Tips for a Smooth Setup

- Keep the Earbuds Close: Ensure the earbuds are close to your device during the pairing process to maintain a strong Bluetooth connection.

- Update Firmware: Check for any firmware updates in the Galaxy Wearable app to ensure your earbuds have the latest features and improvements.

- Fit and Comfort: Try different ear tip sizes to find the most comfortable and secure fit, which also helps with noise cancellation and sound quality.

Pairing with Devices (Samsung, Android, iOS, PC)

Pairing with Samsung Smartphones

1. Open the Charging Case: With the earbuds inside, open the charging case. This will automatically put the earbuds into pairing mode.

2. Enable Bluetooth: On your Samsung smartphone, go to Settings > Connections > Bluetooth and ensure Bluetooth is turned on.

3. Galaxy Wearable App: Open the Galaxy Wearable app. If you don't have it, download it from the Galaxy Store or Google Play Store.

4. Connect: A pop-up should appear on your phone. Tap Connect and follow the on-screen instructions to complete the pairing process.

Pairing with Other Android Devices

1. Open the Charging Case: With the earbuds inside, open the charging case to enter pairing mode.

2. Enable Bluetooth: On your Android device, go to Settings > Bluetooth and turn it on.

3. Select the Earbuds: In the list of available devices, select Galaxy Buds3 Pro to pair.

4. Galaxy Wearable App: For additional features, download the Galaxy Wearable app from the Google Play Store and follow the setup instructions.

Pairing with iPhones

1. Open the Charging Case: With the earbuds inside, open the charging case to enter pairing mode.

2. Enable Bluetooth: On your iPhone, go to Settings > Bluetooth and turn it on.

3. Select the Earbuds: In the list of available devices, select Galaxy Buds3 Pro to pair.

4. Galaxy Buds App: For additional features, download the Galaxy Buds app from the App Store and follow the setup instructions.

Pairing with PCs

1. Open the Charging Case: With the earbuds inside, open the charging case to enter pairing mode.

2. Enable Bluetooth: On your PC, go to Settings > Devices > Bluetooth & other devices and turn on Bluetooth.

3. Add Bluetooth Device: Click Add Bluetooth or other device > Bluetooth.

4. Select the Earbuds: In the list of available devices, select Galaxy Buds3 Pro to pair.

Tips for a Smooth Pairing Process

- Keep Devices Close: Ensure the earbuds and the devices you're pairing with are close to each other.

- Fully Charged: Make sure the earbuds and the charging case are fully charged before starting the pairing process.

- Update Firmware: Check for any firmware updates in the Galaxy Wearable or Galaxy Buds app to ensure the best performance.

- Reset if Needed: If you encounter issues, try resetting the earbuds by placing them in the case and holding the touchpads on both earbuds for about 10 seconds.

PRODUCT OVERVIEW

Design Features of the Samsung Galaxy Buds3 Pro

1. Ergonomic In-Ear Design: The Galaxy Buds3 Pro are designed to fit snugly in your ears, providing comfort even during extended use. The in-ear design helps with noise isolation and enhances sound quality.

Silicone Ear Tips: They come with multiple sizes of silicone ear tips (small, medium, large) to ensure a secure and comfortable fit for different ear sizes.

2. Adaptive Noise Control: This feature uses advanced algorithms to adjust the level of noise cancellation based on your surroundings, allowing you to stay immersed in your audio while remaining aware of important sounds.

3. Dual Drivers: The Buds3 Pro features an independently controlled woofer and tweeter, providing a broad spectrum of sound for a high-resolution audio experience.

4. Touch Controls: The touch-sensitive controls on the earbuds allow you to manage music playback, answer calls, and activate voice assistants with simple taps and gestures.

5. Water and Sweat Resistance: With an IPX7 rating, the Galaxy Buds3 Pro are resistant to water and sweat, making them suitable for workouts and outdoor activities.

6. Compact Charging Case: The sleek and compact charging case not only stores the earbuds but also charges them, providing additional battery life on the go.

Tips for Achieving a Comfortable and Secure Fit

1. Choose the Right Ear Tips:

- Try Different Sizes: Experiment with the small, medium, and large silicone ear tips to find the best fit for your ears. The right size should create a good seal without causing discomfort.

- Proper Insertion: Insert the earbuds into your ears and gently twist them to ensure they are securely in place. The ear tips should fit snugly in your ear canal.

2. Run an Earbud Fit Test:

- Galaxy Wearable App: Use the earbud fit test available in the Galaxy Wearable app to ensure you have the proper fit. The app will guide you through the process and provide feedback on the fit.

3. Adjust for Comfort:

- Rotate the Earbuds: Once inserted, you can rotate the earbuds slightly forward or backward to find the most comfortable position. This also helps in achieving a secure fit.

- Check for Gaps: Ensure there are no gaps between the ear tips and your ear canal, as this can affect sound quality and noise cancellation.

4. Avoid Excessive Pressure:

- Gentle Insertion: Insert the earbuds gently to avoid putting too much pressure on your ears, which can cause discomfort or pain.

- Regular Breaks: If you experience any discomfort, take regular breaks to give your ears a rest.

5. Maintain Cleanliness:

- Clean Ear Tips: Regularly clean the silicone ear tips with a dry, soft cloth to remove any dirt or earwax. This helps maintain hygiene and ensures a good fit.

- Avoid Moisture: Keep the earbuds and ear tips dry to prevent any irritation or damage.

Understanding the LED Indicators

The LED light indicators on the Samsung Galaxy Buds3 Pro earbuds and charging case provide important information about their status.

LED Indicators on the Charging Case

1. Front LED Indicator:

- Green: The charging case is fully charged or has a high battery level.

- Yellow: The charging case has a medium battery level.

- Red: The charging case has a low battery level and needs to be charged soon.

- Flashing Red: There is an error with the charging case or the earbuds. Try resetting the earbuds or checking for any obstructions in the charging contacts.

2. Inside LED Indicators (for each earbud):

- Green: The earbuds are fully charged.

- Yellow: The earbuds are charging and have a medium battery level.

- Red: The earbuds are charging and have a low battery level.

LED Indicators on the Earbuds

1. During Charging:

- Red: The earbuds are currently charging.

- Green: The earbuds are fully charged.

2. During Pairing:

- Flashing Blue: The earbuds are in pairing mode and ready to connect to a device.

Tips for Understanding LED Indicators

- Check Regularly: Regularly check the LED indicators to monitor the battery levels of both the earbuds and the charging case.

- Reset if Needed: If you see a flashing red light indicating an error, try resetting the earbuds by placing them in the case and holding the touchpads on both earbuds for about 10 seconds.

- Keep Contacts Clean: Ensure the charging contacts on both the earbuds and the case are clean to avoid charging issues.

Touch Controls and Gestures

The Samsung Galaxy Buds3 Pro come with a variety of touch control gestures that allow you to manage playback, calls, and activate features like Active Noise Cancellation (ANC).

Playback Controls

1. Single Tap:

- Action: Play or pause music.

- Usage: Tap once on either earbud to start or stop your music.

2. Double Tap:

- Action: Skip to the next track.

- Usage: Tap twice on either earbud to move to the next song in your playlist.

3. Triple Tap:

- Action: Skip back to the previous track.

- Usage: Tap three times on either earbud to go back to the previous song.

Call Controls

1. Single Tap:

- Action: Answer or end a call.

- Usage: Tap once on either earbud to pick up an incoming call or to hang up an ongoing call.

2. Double Tap:

- Action: Decline a call.

- Usage: Tap twice on either earbud to reject an incoming call.

Activating Features

1. Touch and Hold:

- Action: Activate or deactivate Active Noise Cancellation (ANC) or Ambient Sound mode.

- Usage: Touch and hold either earbud to switch between ANC and Ambient Sound mode. You can customize this function in the Galaxy Wearable app.

2. Touch and Hold Both Earbuds (3 seconds):

- Action: Enter Bluetooth pairing mode.

- Usage: Touch and hold both earbuds simultaneously for about 3 seconds to enter pairing mode.

Volume Controls

1. Touch and Hold:

- Action: Adjust the volume.

- Usage: Touch and hold the right earbud to increase the volume, and touch and hold the left earbud to decrease the volume. This function can be customized in the Galaxy Wearable app.

Customizing Touch Controls

1. Galaxy Wearable App:

- Action: Customize touch controls.

- Usage: Open the Galaxy Wearable app, go to Earbud controls, and select Touch and hold. Here, you can assign different functions to the touch and hold gesture for each earbud, such as activating voice assistants or controlling volume.

Tips for Using Touch Controls

- Ensure Proper Fit: Make sure the earbuds fit securely in your ears to avoid accidental touches.

- Clean Touchpads: Keep the touchpads clean and dry for optimal responsiveness.

- Disable Touch Controls: If you find the touch controls too sensitive, you can disable them in the Galaxy Wearable app by enabling the Block touches option.

USING THE BUDS

Playing Music and Managing Calls

Music Playback

1. Play/Pause Music:

Single Tap: Tap once on either earbud to play or pause your music.

2. Skip to the Next Track:

Double Tap: Tap twice on either earbud to skip to the next song.

3. Go Back to the Previous Track:

Triple Tap: Tap three times on either earbud to go back to the previous song.

4. Adjust Volume:

Touch and Hold: Touch and hold the right earbud to increase the volume. Touch and hold the left earbud to decrease the volume. You can customize this function in the Galaxy Wearable app.

Call Management

1. Answer a Call:

Single Tap: Tap once on either earbud to answer an incoming call.

2. End a Call:

Single Tap: Tap once on either earbud to end an ongoing call.

3. Decline a Call:

Double Tap: Tap twice on either earbud to decline an incoming call.

Activating Features

1. Activate/Deactivate Active Noise Cancellation (ANC):

Touch and Hold: Touch and hold either earbud to switch between ANC and Ambient Sound mode. This can be customized in the Galaxy Wearable app.

2. Activate Voice Assistant:

Touch and Hold: You can set the touch and hold gesture to activate your preferred voice assistant (e.g., Bixby, Google Assistant, Siri) through the Galaxy Wearable app.

Customizing Touch Controls

1. Galaxy Wearable App:

Open the App: Open the Galaxy Wearable app on your device.

Select Earbud Controls: Go to Earbud controls and select Touch and hold.

Assign Functions: Customize the touch and hold gesture for each earbud to control volume, activate voice assistants, or switch noise control modes.

Tips for Efficient Use

1. Ensure Proper Fit: Make sure the earbuds fit securely in your ears to avoid accidental touches and ensure optimal sound quality.

2. Keep Touchpads Clean: Regularly clean the touchpads to maintain their responsiveness.

3. Disable Touch Controls: If you find the touch controls too sensitive, you can disable them in the Galaxy Wearable app by enabling the Block touches option.

Activating Noise Cancelation and Transparency Mode

Enabling Active Noise Cancellation (ANC)

1. Using the Touch Controls:

- Touch and Hold: Touch and hold either earbud to activate ANC. You will hear a beep indicating that ANC is turned on.

- Switching Modes: If you continue to touch and hold, the earbuds will cycle through ANC, Ambient Sound mode, and Off. Release the touch when you hear the beep for the desired mode.

2. Using the Galaxy Wearable App:

- Open the App: Launch the Galaxy Wearable app on your smartphone.

- Select Your Earbuds: Tap on your Galaxy Buds3 Pro in the app.

- Noise Control: Go to the Noise control section.

- Activate ANC: Toggle the ANC option to turn it on. You can also adjust the ANC level (High or Low) based on your preference.

Enabling Transparency Mode (Ambient Sound Mode)

1. Using the Touch Controls:

- Touch and Hold: Touch and hold either earbud to switch to Ambient Sound mode. You will hear a beep indicating that Ambient Sound mode is activated.

- Switching Modes: Similar to ANC, continue to touch and hold to cycle through ANC, Ambient Sound mode, and Off. Release the touch when you hear the beep for Ambient Sound mode.

2. Using the Galaxy Wearable App:

- Open the App: Launch the Galaxy Wearable app on your smartphone.

- Select Your Earbuds: Tap on your Galaxy Buds3 Pro in the app.

- Noise Control: Go to the Noise control section.

- Activate Ambient Sound: Toggle the Ambient Sound option to turn it on. You can also adjust the ambient sound volume to your liking.

Tips for Using ANC and Transparency Mode

Adjust Settings: Use the Galaxy Wearable app to fine-tune the levels of ANC and Ambient Sound to suit different environments.

Conversation Mode: Enable the Conversation Detect feature in the Galaxy Wearable app. This feature automatically switches to Ambient Sound mode and lowers the media volume when you start speaking, making it easier to have conversations without removing the earbuds.

Battery Life: Keep in mind that using ANC and Ambient Sound mode can drain the battery faster. Monitor your battery levels and charge the earbuds and case as needed.

Accessing 360 Audio and Adaptive Sound

360 Audio is a feature that provides an immersive sound experience by using head-tracking technology to create a surround sound effect. Here's how you can access and use this feature:

1. Ensure Compatibility:

Device Requirements: Make sure you are using a compatible Samsung Galaxy device running One UI 3.1 or higher.

Update Firmware: Ensure your Galaxy Buds3 Pro and your Samsung device have the latest firmware updates installed.

2. Enable 360 Audio in the Galaxy Wearable App:

Open the App: Launch the Galaxy Wearable app on your Samsung device.

Select Your Earbuds: Tap on your Galaxy Buds3 Pro in the app.

Access Earbud Settings: Go to Earbud settings.

Activate 360 Audio: Find and toggle the 360 Audio option to enable it.

3. Using 360 Audio:

Play Compatible Content: To experience 360 Audio, play content that supports surround sound, such as movies or TV shows with Dolby Atmos or similar formats.

Head Tracking: The 360 Audio feature uses head-tracking technology to adjust the sound based on your head movements, making it feel like the sound is coming from fixed points around you.

Benefits of 360 Audio for Sound Immersion

1. Enhanced Immersion:

Surround Sound Effect: 360 Audio creates a 360-degree sound field, making you feel like you are in the middle of the action. This is particularly effective for movies, games, and virtual reality experiences.

2. Realistic Audio Experience:

Head Tracking: The head-tracking technology ensures that the sound adjusts dynamically as you move your head, maintaining the illusion that the sound sources are fixed in space.

3. Improved Spatial Awareness:

Directional Sound: By simulating the directionality of sound, 360 Audio helps you better perceive where sounds are coming from, enhancing your overall listening experience.

ADVANCED FEATURES

Seamless Device Switching

Seamlessly switching your Samsung Galaxy Buds3 Pro between different devices in the Samsung ecosystem is made easy with the Auto Switch feature.

Using Auto Switch

1. Ensure Compatibility:

- Device Requirements: Auto Switch is available on Samsung phones, tablets, and Samsung TVs from 2022 and later. Ensure your devices are compatible and running One UI 3.1 or higher.

2. Pair Your Devices:

- Initial Pairing: Make sure your Galaxy Buds3 Pro are paired with all the Samsung devices you want to switch between. You can do this through the Bluetooth settings on each device.

3. Enable Auto Switch:

- Galaxy Wearable App: Open the Galaxy Wearable app on your Samsung device.

- Select Your Earbuds: Tap on your Galaxy Buds3 Pro in the app.

- Auto Switch Settings: Go to Earbud settings and find the Auto Switch option. Toggle it on.

Switching Between Devices

1. Automatic Switching:

- Incoming Calls: If you are listening to music on your Galaxy tablet and receive a call on your Samsung phone, the earbuds will automatically switch to the phone so you can take the call.

- Media Playback: When you stop using one device and start playing media on another paired Samsung device, the earbuds will automatically switch to the new device.

2. Manual Switching:

- Bluetooth Settings: If automatic switching doesn't occur, you can manually switch by going to the Bluetooth settings on the device you want to connect to and selecting the Galaxy Buds3 Pro from the list of paired devices.

Tips for Seamless Switching

- Keep Bluetooth On: Ensure Bluetooth is enabled on all your Samsung devices to facilitate seamless switching.

- Stay Within Range: Keep your devices within Bluetooth range (about 10 meters) to maintain a stable connection.

- Update Firmware: Regularly check for firmware updates for both your earbuds and Samsung devices to ensure optimal performance and compatibility.

How to Enable Game Mode on the Samsung Galaxy Buds3 Pro

Game Mode is designed to reduce audio latency, providing a more synchronized and immersive experience, especially useful for gaming and watching videos. Here's how to enable it:

1. Open the Galaxy Wearable App:

Launch the App: Open the Galaxy Wearable app on your Samsung device. If you don't have it, download it from the Galaxy Store or Google Play Store.

2. Select Your Earbuds:

Connect: Ensure your Galaxy Buds3 Pro are connected to your device.

Navigate to Settings: Tap on your Galaxy Buds3 Pro in the app to access their settings.

3. Access Labs:

Find Labs: Scroll down and select the Labs section within the app. This section contains experimental features, including Game Mode.

4. Enable Game Mode:

Toggle On: Find the Game Mode option and toggle it on. This will activate low-latency mode, reducing the delay between audio and video.

Benefits of Game Mode for Low-Latency Audio

1. Reduced Audio Lag:

Synchronization: Game Mode minimizes the delay between the audio you hear and the action you see on screen, providing a more synchronized experience. This is crucial for gaming, where timing can impact performance.

2. Enhanced Gaming Experience:

Immersion: By reducing latency, Game Mode helps create a more immersive gaming environment, making it easier to react to in-game sounds and cues in real-time.

3. Improved Video Watching:

Seamless Playback: When watching videos, Game Mode ensures that the audio matches the video perfectly, preventing any distracting delays that can disrupt your viewing experience.

Tips for Using Game Mode

- Battery Considerations: Keep in mind that enabling Game Mode may slightly increase battery consumption. Monitor your battery levels and charge the earbuds and case as needed.

- Device Compatibility: Ensure your Samsung device is compatible and running the latest software updates to fully support Game Mode.

- Switching Modes: You can easily toggle Game Mode on and off in the Galaxy Wearable app, allowing you to switch back to standard mode when low latency is not required.

Real-Time Language Translation Capabilities of the Samsung Galaxy Buds3 Pro

The Samsung Galaxy Buds3 Pro come equipped with an advanced real-time language translation feature, powered by Galaxy AI. This feature allows you to understand and communicate in different languages seamlessly, making it ideal for travel, international business, and multilingual environments.

Key Features

1. Listening Mode: This mode is designed for one-way translation, perfect for situations like guided tours, foreign language lectures, and international conferences.

How It Works: The Galaxy Buds3 Pro will listen to the speech in a foreign language and translate it into your preferred language, delivering the translation directly to your earbuds.

2. Conversation Mode: This mode facilitates two-way translation, enabling real-time conversations with people who speak different languages.

How It Works: The earbuds use Galaxy AI to translate both sides of the conversation. You can speak in your language, and the translation will be played through your phone's speaker for the other person. Their response will be translated back to you through the earbuds.

How to Activate and Use Real-Time Translation

1. Initial Setup:

Ensure Connection: Make sure your Galaxy Buds3 Pro are connected to your Samsung device via Bluetooth.

Download the Interpreter App: If not already installed, download the Interpreter app from the Galaxy Store or Google Play Store.

2. Using the Interpreter App:

Open the App: Launch the Interpreter app on your connected Samsung device.

Select Mode: Choose between Listening Mode (single chat bubble icon) and Conversation Mode (double chat bubble icon).

Select Languages: Choose the languages you want to translate between. For example, select English as your language and Spanish as the target language.

3. Activating Translation:

Listening Mode: Tap the microphone icon in the app to start listening. The app will translate the spoken language and deliver it to your earbuds.

Conversation Mode: Tap the microphone icon to start a conversation. Speak into your phone, and the app will translate your speech and play it through the phone's speaker. The other person's response will be translated back to you through the earbuds.

4. Using Touch Controls:

Pause/Resume Translation: You can pause and resume the translation using the touch controls on the earbuds. Pinch an earbud to pause and pinch again to resume.

Benefits of Real-Time Translation

1. Seamless Communication:

Real-Time Interaction: Enables smooth and natural conversations without language barriers, making it easier to communicate in multilingual settings.

2. Convenience:

Hands-Free Operation: The translation is delivered directly to your earbuds, allowing you to keep your hands free for other tasks.

3. Enhanced Travel Experience:

Understanding Local Languages: Helps you navigate foreign countries, understand local guides, and interact with locals more effectively.

CUSTOMIZATION VIA THE GALAXY WEARABLE APP

Adjusting the Equalizer

Steps on how to use the Galaxy Wearable app to adjust the Equalizer settings for your Samsung Galaxy Buds3 Pro:

1. Download and Open the Galaxy Wearable App:

Install the App: If you haven't already, download the Galaxy Wearable app from the Galaxy Store or Google Play Store.

Launch the App: Open the app on your Samsung device.

2. Connect Your Galaxy Buds3 Pro:

Pair the Earbuds: Ensure your Galaxy Buds3 Pro are connected to your device via Bluetooth. Open the charging case to put the earbuds in pairing mode, and follow the on-screen instructions in the app to connect them.

3. Access the Equalizer Settings:

Open Earbud Settings: Once connected, tap on your Galaxy Buds3 Pro in the app to access their settings.

46

Select Equalizer: Navigate to the Equalizer section. This is usually found under Earbud settings or directly on the home screen of the app.

4. Choose an Equalizer Preset:

Preset Options: You will see several preset options such as Normal, Bass boost, Soft, Dynamic, Clear, and Treble boost. Each preset adjusts the sound profile to enhance different aspects of the audio.

Select a Preset: Tap on the preset that best suits your listening preference. You can switch between presets to find the one you like the most.

Benefits of Using the Equalizer

1. Personalized Sound Experience:

Customization: The Equalizer allows you to tailor the sound to your liking, whether you prefer more bass, clearer vocals, or a balanced sound profile.

2. Enhanced Audio Quality:

Optimized Sound: By adjusting the Equalizer settings, you can optimize the audio quality for different types of content, such as music, podcasts, or movies.

3. Improved Listening Comfort:

Adapt to Environment: Different environments may require different sound settings. For example, you might prefer a bass boost in noisy environments or a softer sound in quiet settings.

Tips for Using the Equalizer

- Experiment with Presets: Try out different presets to see which one enhances your listening experience the most.

- Update Firmware: Ensure your Galaxy Buds3 Pro and the Galaxy Wearable app are updated to the latest firmware for the best performance and access to the latest features.

- Use with Different Content: Adjust the Equalizer settings based on the type of content you are listening to for an optimal audio experience.

Enabling and Configuring 360 Audio

Steps on how to enable and configure 360 Audio on your Samsung Galaxy Buds3 Pro using the Galaxy Wearable app:

1. Ensure Compatibility:

Device Requirements: Make sure you are using a compatible Samsung Galaxy device running One UI 3.1 or higher. This feature works with devices like the Galaxy S21 series, Galaxy Tab S7, and newer models.

2. Update Firmware:

Check for Updates: Ensure that both your Galaxy Buds3 Pro and your Samsung device have the latest firmware updates installed. You can check for updates in the Galaxy Wearable app under Earbud settings > Earbuds software update.

3. Open the Galaxy Wearable App:

Launch the App: Open the Galaxy Wearable app on your Samsung device. If you don't have it, download it from the Galaxy Store or Google Play Store.

4. Connect Your Galaxy Buds3 Pro:

Pair the Earbuds: Ensure your Galaxy Buds3 Pro are connected to your device via Bluetooth. Open the charging case to put the earbuds in pairing mode, and follow the on-screen instructions in the app to connect them.

5. Access 360 Audio Settings:

 Navigate to Settings: Tap on your Galaxy Buds3 Pro in the app to access their settings.

Select 360 Audio: Scroll down and find the 360 Audio option. Tap on it to access the settings.

6. Enable 360 Audio:

Toggle On: Toggle the 360 Audio switch to enable the feature. You will see a confirmation message indicating that 360 Audio is now active.

7. Configure 360 Audio:

Head Tracking: Ensure that head tracking is enabled. This feature uses the sensors in your earbuds to adjust the sound based on your head movements, providing a more immersive experience.

Benefits of 360 Audio

1. Enhanced Immersion:

Surround Sound Effect: 360 Audio creates a 360-degree sound field, making you feel like you are in the middle of the action. This is particularly effective for movies, games, and virtual reality experiences.

2. Realistic Audio Experience:

Head Tracking: The head-tracking technology ensures that the sound adjusts dynamically as you move your head, maintaining the illusion that the sound sources are fixed in space.

3. Improved Spatial Awareness:

Directional Sound: By simulating the directionality of sound, 360 Audio helps you better perceive where sounds are coming from, enhancing your overall listening experience.

Managing Notifications and Settings

Steps on how to manage notifications for your Samsung Galaxy Buds3 Pro using the Galaxy Wearable app:

1. Download and Open the Galaxy Wearable App:

Install the App: If you haven't already, download the Galaxy Wearable app from the Galaxy Store or Google Play Store.

Launch the App: Open the app on your Samsung device.

2. Connect Your Galaxy Buds3 Pro:

Pair the Earbuds: Ensure your Galaxy Buds3 Pro are connected to your device via Bluetooth. Open the charging case to put the earbuds in pairing mode, and follow the on-screen instructions in the app to connect them.

3. Access Notification Settings:

Open Earbud Settings: Once connected, tap on your Galaxy Buds3 Pro in the app to access their settings.

Select Notifications: Navigate to the Notifications section within the app.

4. Enable Notifications:

Toggle Notifications On: Ensure that the notification toggle is turned on to allow notifications to be sent to your earbuds.

5. Customize Notification Preferences:

Select Apps: You can choose which apps you want to receive notifications from. Tap on Manage notifications to see a list of installed apps.

Toggle Apps On/Off: Toggle the switch next to each app to enable or disable notifications for that specific app.

6. Voice Notifications:

Enable Voice Notifications: If you want to hear notifications read aloud, enable the Voice notifications option. This feature will read out the content of notifications through your earbuds.

Benefits of Managing Notifications

1. Stay Informed:

Real-Time Alerts: Receive important notifications directly in your ears without needing to check your phone, keeping you informed while on the go.

2. Customization:

Selective Notifications: Customize which apps can send notifications to your earbuds, ensuring you only receive alerts from the most important apps.

3. Hands-Free Operation:

Voice Notifications: With voice notifications, you can stay updated on messages, calls, and other alerts without having to look at your device.

Tips for Managing Notifications

Prioritize Important Apps: Enable notifications for essential apps like messaging, email, and calendar, and disable less important ones to avoid unnecessary interruptions.

Adjust Notification Volume: Ensure the notification volume is set to a comfortable level in the Galaxy Wearable app.

Update Firmware: Regularly check for firmware updates for both your earbuds and the Galaxy Wearable app to ensure optimal performance and access to the latest features.

MAINTENANCE AND CARE

Cleaning and Storing the Earbuds

Keeping your Samsung Galaxy Buds3 Pro clean is essential for maintaining optimal performance and hygiene. How to clean your earbuds and charging case:

Cleaning the Earbuds

1. Remove the Ear Tips:

Detach Carefully: Gently remove the silicone ear tips from the earbuds. This will give you better access to the speaker mesh and other parts.

2. Clean the Ear Tips:

Wash with Water: Rinse the silicone ear tips with warm water. Avoid using soap or harsh chemicals.

Dry Completely: Ensure the ear tips are completely dry before reattaching them to the earbuds.

3. Clean the Speaker Mesh:

Use a Dry Brush: Use a soft, dry brush (like a toothbrush) to gently remove any debris or earwax from the speaker mesh.

Avoid Liquids: Do not use liquids to clean the speaker mesh to prevent damage.

4. Clean the Earbud Surface:

Wipe with a Cloth: Use a dry, soft cloth to wipe the surface of the earbuds. Avoid using alcohol or soapy water.

Cleaning the Charging Case

1. Clean the Charging Contacts:

Use a Cotton Swab: Gently clean the charging contacts inside the case and on the earbuds with a dry cotton swab. This helps maintain a good connection for charging.

2. Clean the Case Interior:

Remove Debris: Use a dry brush or a soft cloth to remove any dust or debris from the inside of the case.

Avoid Liquids: Do not use liquids to clean the inside of the case to prevent any damage.

3. Clean the Case Exterior:

Wipe with a Cloth: Use a dry, soft cloth to clean the exterior of the charging case. If necessary, slightly dampen the cloth with water, but ensure the case is completely dry before using it again.

Tips for Maintaining Optimal Performance

1. Regular Cleaning:

Frequency: Clean your earbuds and charging case regularly, especially if you use them frequently or during workouts.

2. Proper Storage:

Use the Case: Always store your earbuds in the charging case when not in use to protect them from dust and damage.

3. Avoid Extreme Conditions:

Temperature and Humidity: Keep your earbuds and case away from extreme temperatures and high humidity to prevent damage.

4. Check for Updates:

Firmware Updates: Regularly check for firmware updates in the Galaxy Wearable app to ensure your earbuds have the latest features and improvements.

Replacing Ear Tips

Proper storage of your Samsung Galaxy Buds3 Pro and charging case is essential for maintaining their durability and performance.

Tips for Storing the Galaxy Buds3 Pro and Charging Case

1. Use the Charging Case:

Primary Storage: Always store your earbuds in the charging case when not in use. This protects them from dust, dirt, and physical damage.

Charging: Keeping the earbuds in the case also ensures they are charged and ready for use whenever you need them.

2. Keep the Case Closed:

Protection: Make sure the charging case is closed when storing the earbuds. This prevents debris from entering the case and keeps the earbuds secure.

3. Avoid Extreme Temperatures:

Temperature Control: Store the earbuds and case in a cool, dry place. Avoid exposing them to extreme temperatures (both hot and cold) as this can damage the battery and other components.

4. Avoid Humidity:

Dry Environment: Keep the earbuds and case away from high humidity environments, such as bathrooms or kitchens, to prevent moisture damage.

5. Use a Carrying Pouch:

Additional Protection: If you have a carrying pouch, use it to store the charging case. This provides extra protection against scratches and impacts, especially when traveling.

6. Regular Cleaning:

Maintain Cleanliness: Regularly clean the earbuds and charging case to remove any dust or debris. Use a dry, soft cloth for the exterior and a dry brush or cotton swab for the charging contacts.

7. Avoid Overloading:

No Heavy Pressure: Do not place heavy objects on top of the charging case or earbuds. Excessive pressure can damage the case and the earbuds inside.

8. Check Battery Levels:

Monitor Battery: Ensure the earbuds and case are sufficiently charged before storing them for extended periods. This helps maintain battery health.

Safety Tips

Here are some important safety precautions to follow when using and maintaining your Samsung Galaxy Buds3 Pro:

General Usage

1. Proper Fit:

Use Correct Ear Tips: Ensure you use the ear tips that fit your ears properly to avoid discomfort and ensure optimal sound quality.

Avoid Excessive Pressure: Do not insert the earbuds too deeply or apply excessive pressure, as this can cause ear discomfort or damage.

2. Volume Levels:

Moderate Volume: Keep the volume at a moderate level to prevent hearing damage. Avoid listening at high volumes for extended periods.

3. Awareness of Surroundings:

Stay Alert: Be aware of your surroundings, especially when using the earbuds outdoors or while moving, to avoid accidents.

Maintenance and Cleaning

1. Regular Cleaning:

Clean Ear Tips and Mesh: Regularly clean the ear tips and speaker mesh with a dry, soft cloth to remove earwax and debris.

Avoid Liquids: Do not use water or cleaning agents directly on the earbuds or charging case to prevent damage.

2. Charging Contacts:

Keep Contacts Clean: Ensure the charging contacts on both the earbuds and the case are clean to maintain efficient charging.

Storage

1. Use the Charging Case:

Store Properly: Always store the earbuds in the charging case when not in use to protect them from dust and damage.

Keep Case Closed: Ensure the charging case is closed to prevent debris from entering.

2. Avoid Extreme Conditions:

Temperature and Humidity: Store the earbuds and case in a cool, dry place. Avoid exposing them to extreme temperatures and high humidity.

Handling

1. Avoid Dropping:

Handle with Care: Be careful not to drop the earbuds or the charging case, as this can cause physical damage.

2. Avoid Contact with Liquids:

Water Resistance: While the earbuds have some water resistance, avoid submerging them in water or exposing them to excessive moisture.

Health Precautions

1. Discontinue Use if Discomfort Occurs:

Ear Pain or Irritation: If you experience any ear pain, discomfort, or skin irritation while using the earbuds, discontinue use immediately and consult a doctor.

TROUBLESHOOTING AND SUPPORT

Common Issues and Solutions

Here are some common issues you might encounter with the Samsung Galaxy Buds3 Pro and step-by-step solutions for troubleshooting them:

1. Earbuds Not Charging

Issue: The earbuds are not charging when placed in the charging case.

Solution:

- Check the Charging Contacts: Ensure the charging contacts on both the earbuds and the case are clean. Use a dry cotton swab to clean them if necessary.

- Proper Placement: Make sure the earbuds are properly placed in the charging case and the lid is closed securely.

- Charge the Case: Connect the charging case to a power source using the USB-C cable. Ensure the case itself is charged.

- Reset the Earbuds: Place the earbuds in the case, close the lid, wait for at least 7 seconds, then take them out again.

2. Connectivity Issues

Issue: The earbuds are not connecting to your device or frequently disconnect.

Solution:

- Bluetooth Settings: Ensure Bluetooth is enabled on your device. Turn Bluetooth off and on again to reset the connection.

- Re-Pair the Earbuds: Remove the Galaxy Buds3 Pro from your device's Bluetooth list. Then, re-pair them by opening the charging case and following the pairing instructions.

- Update Firmware: Check for firmware updates in the Galaxy Wearable app and install any available updates.

- Reset the Earbuds: In the Galaxy Wearable app, go to Earbud settings > Reset to reset the earbuds to their factory settings.

3. Audio Issues

Issue: Poor sound quality, low volume, or no sound from one or both earbuds.

Solution:

- Check Volume Levels: Ensure the volume on your device is turned up and not muted.

- Clean the Earbuds: Clean the speaker mesh with a dry, soft brush to remove any debris or earwax that might be blocking the sound.

- Adjust Fit: Make sure the earbuds fit snugly in your ears. Try different ear tip sizes for a better fit and improved sound quality.

- Update Firmware: Ensure your earbuds have the latest firmware updates installed via the Galaxy Wearable app.

4. Touch Controls Not Responding

Issue: The touch controls on the earbuds are unresponsive.

Solution:

- Clean the Touchpads: Wipe the touchpads with a dry, soft cloth to ensure they are clean and free of any debris.

- Check Fit: Make sure the earbuds are properly seated in your ears, as the touch sensors need to be in contact with your skin.

- Reset the Earbuds: Place the earbuds in the charging case, close the lid, wait for at least 7 seconds, then take them out again.

- Enable Touch Controls: In the Galaxy Wearable app, go to Earbud settings > Touch controls and ensure the touch controls are enabled.

5. Battery Draining Quickly

Issue: The battery life of the earbuds or charging case is shorter than expected.

Solution:

- Disable Unused Features: Turn off features like ANC (Active Noise Cancellation) and Ambient Sound mode when not needed, as they consume more battery.

- Check for Updates: Ensure your earbuds and the Galaxy Wearable app are updated to the latest firmware.

- Proper Charging: Make sure the earbuds and case are fully charged before use. Avoid overcharging by disconnecting them once fully charged.

Resetting the Buds

Resetting your Samsung Galaxy Buds3 Pro to factory settings can help resolve various issues and restore them to their original state. Here are the steps :

1. Open the Galaxy Wearable App:

Launch the App: Open the Galaxy Wearable app on your connected Samsung device. If you don't have it, download it from the Galaxy Store or Google Play Store.

2. Connect Your Earbuds:

Ensure Connection: Make sure your Galaxy Buds3 Pro are connected to your device via Bluetooth. Open the charging case to put the earbuds in pairing mode if they are not already connected.

3. Access Earbud Settings:

Select Your Earbuds: Tap on your Galaxy Buds3 Pro in the app to access their settings.

Navigate to General: Scroll down and select the General section.

4. Reset the Earbuds:

Find Reset Option: In the General section, tap on Reset.

Confirm Reset: You will be prompted to confirm the reset. Tap Reset again to confirm. This will reset your earbuds to their factory settings.

Alternative Method (Manual Reset)

If you are unable to access the Galaxy Wearable app, you can manually reset the earbuds:

1. Place Earbuds in the Case:

Insert Earbuds: Place both earbuds in the charging case and close the lid.

2. Wait and Reset:

Hold Touchpads: Open the lid, then touch and hold the touchpads on both earbuds for about 10 seconds until the LED indicators flash red, green, and blue. This indicates that the earbuds have been reset.

After Resetting

1. Re-Pair the Earbuds:

Pair Again: After resetting, you will need to pair the earbuds with your device again. Open the charging case to put the earbuds in pairing mode and follow the pairing instructions in the Galaxy Wearable app or your device's Bluetooth settings.

2. Reconfigure Settings:

Customize Settings: Any custom settings or preferences you had set up will be erased. You will need to reconfigure these settings in the Galaxy Wearable app.

Contacting Samsung Support

If you encounter issues with your Samsung Galaxy Buds3 Pro and need assistance, you can contact Samsung customer support through various channels. Here's how you can reach them:

Contacting Samsung Customer Support

1. Phone Support:

Samsung Support Hotline: You can call Samsung's customer support at 1-800-SAMSUNG (726-7864) for assistance with your Galaxy Buds3 Pro.

2. Online Support:

Samsung Support Website: Visit the [Samsung Support website](https://www.samsung.com/us/support/mobile/audi o/wireless-earbuds/galaxy-buds/) to find solutions, resources, and contact options.

Live Chat: Use the live chat feature on the Samsung Support website to get real-time assistance from a support representative.

3. Samsung Members App:

In-App Support: Download the Samsung Members app on your mobile device. The app provides access to customer support, including live chat, troubleshooting guides, and community forums.

4. Service Centers:

Find a Service Center: You can locate a nearby Samsung service center for in-person assistance. Use the [service center locator](https://www.samsung.com/us/support/service/locat ion) on the Samsung website to find the nearest center.

5. Email Support:

Submit a Request: You can also submit a support request via email through the Samsung Support website. Provide detailed information about your issue to receive a response from a support representative.

TECHNICAL SPECIFICATIONS

Here are the technical specifications for the Samsung Galaxy Buds3 Pro:

Battery Life

Earbuds: Up to 6 hours with Active Noise Cancellation (ANC) on, and up to 7 hours with ANC off.

Charging Case: Provides an additional 20 hours with ANC on, and up to 23 hours with ANC off, totaling up to 26 hours with ANC on and 30 hours with ANC off.

Audio Features

Active Noise Cancellation (ANC): Reduces ambient noise for a more immersive listening experience.

Ambient Sound Mode: Allows you to hear your surroundings while listening to audio.

360 Audio: Provides a surround sound experience with head-tracking technology.

Dual Drivers: Enhanced 2-way speaker system for improved sound quality.

Connectivity Options

Bluetooth Version: 5.4, supporting SBC, AAC, and SSC codecs.

Seamless Device Switching: Automatically switches between Samsung devices within the ecosystem.

Water Resistance Rating

IP57: Dust and water-resistant, suitable for workouts and outdoor use.

Physical Specifications

Earbud Dimensions: 18.1 x 19.8 x 33.2 mm.

Earbud Weight: 5.4 grams per earbud.

Charging Case Dimensions: 58.9 x 48.7 x 24.4 mm.

Charging Case Weight: 46.5 grams.

WARRANTY AND SERVICE INFORMATION

Warranty Coverage for the Samsung Galaxy Buds3 Pro

The Samsung Galaxy Buds3 Pro comes with a standard limited warranty that covers manufacturing defects and issues that arise under normal use. Here are the key details:

1. Warranty Period:

- Duration: Typically, the warranty period is 12 months from the date of purchase.

- Coverage: The warranty covers defects in materials and workmanship. It does not cover damage caused by misuse, accidents, or unauthorized modifications.

2. Samsung Care+:

- Extended Coverage: Samsung offers an optional extended warranty service called Samsung Care+. This service provides additional coverage for accidental damage, including drops and spills, beyond the standard warranty.

- Enrollment: You can enroll in Samsung Care+ at the time of purchase or within a specified period after purchase.

How to Claim Warranty Services

If you encounter an issue with your Galaxy Buds3 Pro that you believe is covered under the warranty, follow these steps to claim warranty services:

1. Verify Warranty Status:

- Check Online: Visit the [Samsung Warranty Check](https://www.samsung.com/us/support/warranty/) page and enter your product's serial number or IMEI to verify the warranty status.

- Samsung Members App: You can also check the warranty status through the Samsung Members app by logging in and navigating to your registered products.

2. Contact Samsung Support:

- Phone Support: Call Samsung customer support at 1-800-SAMSUNG (726-7864) for assistance.

- Live Chat: Use the live chat feature on the [Samsung Support website](https://www.samsung.com/us/support/) to get real-time help from a support representative.

- Email Support: Submit a support request via email through the Samsung Support website.

3. Visit a Service Center:

- Locate a Service Center: Use the [service center locator](https://www.samsung.com/us/support/service/location) on the Samsung website to find the nearest authorized service center.

- In-Person Assistance: Bring your Galaxy Buds3 Pro and proof of purchase to the service center for in-person assistance.

4. Submit a Repair Request:

- Online Request: You can submit a repair request online through the Samsung Support website. Navigate to the Repair Service page and follow the instructions to request service.

- Samsung Care+ Claims: If you have Samsung Care+, you can start a claim by visiting the [Samsung Care+ portal](https://samsung-us.servify.tech/mycare) or calling the dedicated support line.

Tips for a Smooth Warranty Claim Process

- Keep Proof of Purchase: Always keep your receipt or proof of purchase, as it may be required to validate your warranty claim.

- Register Your Product: Register your Galaxy Buds3 Pro on the Samsung website or through the Samsung Members app to streamline the warranty claim process.

- Follow Instructions: Carefully follow the instructions provided by Samsung support representatives to ensure a smooth and efficient resolution to your issue.

FAQs

Frequently Asked Questions (FAQs) about the Samsung Galaxy Buds3 Pro

1. How do I pair the Galaxy Buds3 Pro with my device?

Solution:

- Open the case with the earbuds inside and ensure Bluetooth is enabled on your device.

- For Samsung devices, a pop-up will appear for pairing. Tap Connect.

- For non-Samsung devices, search for "Galaxy Buds3 Pro" in the Bluetooth settings and select it.

- Tip: If pairing fails, reset the earbuds by placing them in the case, holding the touch panels for 10 seconds, and trying again.

2. How do I activate and adjust Active Noise Cancelation (ANC)?

Solution:

- Touch and hold either earbud to toggle between ANC, Transparency Mode, and Off.

- Use the Galaxy Wearable app to adjust the intensity of ANC for more control.

- Tip: For optimal noise cancelation, ensure the earbuds fit snugly using the correct ear tip size.

3. How do I update the firmware of the Galaxy Buds3 Pro?

Solution:

- Open the Galaxy Wearable app.

- Navigate to Earbuds Settings > Earbuds Software Update > Download and Install.

- Tip: Keep your earbuds connected to the app during the update, and ensure they have sufficient battery charge.

4. How do I reset the Galaxy Buds3 Pro to factory settings?

Solution:

- Open the Galaxy Wearable app and go to Earbuds Settings.

- Tap Reset Earbuds and confirm your action.

- Tip: A reset resolves most connection and functionality issues but will erase custom settings.

5. Why is the sound uneven between the earbuds?

Solution:

- Ensure both earbuds are clean and free from debris.

- Use the Galaxy Wearable app to adjust the sound balance under accessibility settings.

- Tip: Uneven sound may occur if one earbud's battery is lower than the other. Charge both earbuds fully.

6. What should I do if the touch controls don't respond?

Solution:

- Clean the touch surface with a dry, lint-free cloth.

- Ensure touch controls are enabled in the Galaxy Wearable app under Touch Controls.

- Tip: Avoid excessive moisture or sweat on the touch-sensitive areas to maintain responsiveness.

7. How do I enable 360 Audio and what does it do?

Solution:

- In the Galaxy Wearable app, go to Labs and enable 360 Audio.

- Wear both earbuds, and enjoy an immersive surround sound experience with compatible content.

- Tip: For the best experience, use a Samsung Galaxy device running Android 11 or later.

8. How long does the battery last on the Galaxy Buds3 Pro?

Answer:

- With ANC on, the earbuds last approximately 5 hours (18 hours with the case).

- With ANC off, they last around 8 hours (29 hours with the case).

- Tip: Use fast charging for a quick 5-minute charge that gives up to 1 hour of playback.

9. Are the Galaxy Buds3 Pro water-resistant?

Answer:

- Yes, they have an IP57 rating, making them dust-resistant and water-resistant to submersion in up to 1 meter of water for 30 minutes.

- Tip: Avoid using them in high-pressure water environments like showers or swimming.

10. How do I clean and maintain the earbuds?

Solution:

- Use a dry, soft brush or a cotton swab to clean the mesh and charging contacts.

- Avoid using liquids or compressed air directly on the earbuds.

- Tip: Regular cleaning ensures optimal performance and sound quality.

11. Can I use one earbud at a time?

Answer:

- Yes, the Galaxy Buds3 Pro supports single-earbud use. Simply remove one earbud from the case and use it while the other charges.

- Tip: Single-earbud mode is ideal for calls or when you need to stay aware of your surroundings.

12. How do I fix connection issues with the Galaxy Buds3 Pro?

Solution:

- Reset the earbuds as described earlier.

- Forget the device from your Bluetooth list and pair it again.

- Ensure the earbuds and device are within the recommended range (10 meters).

- Tip: Turn off nearby Bluetooth devices that might cause interference.

www.ingramcontent.com/pod-product-compliance
Lightning Source LLC
Chambersburg PA
CBHW071028050326
40689CB00014B/3569